Exploring the Universe

Giles Sparrow

WORLD ALMANAC® LIBRARY

Please visit our web site at: www.garethstevens.com
For a free color catalog describing World Almanac® Library's list of high-quality books
and multimedia programs, call 1-800-848-2928 (USA) or 1-800-387-3178 (Canada).
World Almanac® Library's fax: (414) 332-3567.

Library of Congress Cataloging-in-Publication Data

Sparrow, Giles.
      Exploring the universe / by Giles Sparrow.
         p. cm. — (Secrets of the universe)
      Includes bibliographical references and index.
      ISBN-10: 0-8368-7276-2 — ISBN-13: 978-0-8368-7276-7 (lib. bdg.)
      ISBN-10: 0-8368-7283-5 — ISBN-10: 978-0-8368-7283-5 (softcover)
    1. Outer space—Exploration—Juvenile literature. 2. Space vehicles—Juvenile literature.
  I. Title. II. Series: Sparrow, Giles. Secrets of the universe. III. Series.
  QB500.262.S64   2007
  919.904—dc22   2006009955

This North American edition first published in 2007 by
World Almanac® Library
A Member of the WRC Media Family of Companies
330 West Olive Street, Suite 100
Milwaukee, WI 53212 USA

Amber Books project editor: James Bennett
Amber Books design: Richard Mason
Amber Books picture research: Terry Forshaw

World Almanac® Library editor: Carol Ryback
World Almanac® Library designer: Scott M. Krall
World Almanac® Library art direction: Tammy West
World Almanac® Library production: Jessica Morris and Robert Kraus

Picture acknowledgments: All photographs courtesy of NASA except for the following:
CORBIS: 9 (Bettmann). All artworks courtesy of International Masters Publishers Ltd.

CONTENTS

Cover and title page: Earth hangs off the horizon as the cockpit portion of *Apollo 11*'s lunar module *Eagle* rises off the lunar surface. Astronauts Neil Armstrong and Edwin "Buzz" Aldrin soon rejoined fellow astronaut Michael Collins in the *Columbia* command module after their historic first Moon landing in July 1969.

CHAPTER 1

GETTING INTO SPACE

Humans have always been fascinated by the idea of traveling into space. The earliest recorded story of a journey to the Moon dates from Roman times. The author Lucian of Samosata, who wrote in the second century A.D., had his hero carried to the Moon on a giant waterspout. Trips into space were a popular subject for romantic fantasies as early as medieval times, but it was only in the 1800s that a few people began to take the subject more seriously.

The great French science-fiction writer Jules Verne (1828–1905) wrote *From the Earth to the Moon* in 1865, while British writer H. G. Wells (1866–1946) wrote *The First Men in the Moon* in 1901.

Both novels had a huge influence on the pioneers of real space travel in the 1900s, but both made basic scientific errors. Verne's heroes were blasted to the Moon in a capsule fired from a huge cannon (the acceleration would have killed them), while the lunar ship Wells wrote about used plates of a special (and impossible) material to shield it from gravity. Both authors were rightly trying to overcome the problems of traveling through a vacuum. The French writer Cyrano de Bergerac had already suggested the best practical solution to space travel—the rocket—in the 1600s.

Rocket pioneers

Rockets have been around for centuries in the form of fireworks and weapons, but the first person to take them seriously as a means of space travel was Russian schoolteacher Konstantin Tsiolkovsky. Although he did not conduct any experiments, he worked out the principles of rocketry that are used to this day. For example, he realized that a rocket's flight path could be altered using vanes that deflect the exhaust gases as they leave the rocket. He also discovered the benefits of the multistage rocket. This is a stack of two

Friendship 7, **launched on February 20, 1962, carried astronaut John Glenn Jr., who became the first American to orbit Earth.**

WHY ROCKETS?

Most propulsion systems on Earth rely on pushing against something, such as air, water, or the ground. Space is a vacuum, so there is nothing to push against. A rocket, however, can get around this major problem of space travel because it pushes against itself. It relies on Isaac Newton's (1642–1726) third law of motion, which states that "for every action, there is an equal and opposite reaction." Firework rockets are packed with an explosive mixture that reacts (or combusts) with oxygen in the air. As exhaust gases are pushed out the back of the rocket at high speed, the rocket is pushed in the opposite direction of the escaping gases.

Rockets intended to travel outside the atmosphere cannot rely on combustion with the air around them, so they must carry two different chemicals: a fuel or propellant and an "oxidant." The oxidant plays the same role as the oxygen that comes from the air. In solid-fuel rockets (such as the boosters on the space shuttle), these two chemicals are mixed together and packed into a tube. They burn fiercely when ignited, and gas escapes through a nozzle at the base. In liquid-fuel rockets, the fuel and oxidant are stored in separate tanks. They are mixed together and ignited in small, controllable amounts inside the rocket engine during takeoff or flight.

or more self-contained rocket engines that ignite one at a time and fall away as their fuel is exhausted. This allows the lighter upper stages to continue into space without having to drag the empty fuel tanks behind them.

Tsiolkovsky's 1896 book was ignored until after the 1917 Russian Revolution. By then, a new generation of scientists was experimenting with rockets. In the United States, Robert Goddard (*see box, page 7*) flew the first liquid-fueled rocket in 1926. Both Tsiolkovsky and Goddard inspired the foundation of rocketry societies in several countries.

VfR, the German rocket society, *Verein für Raumschiffahrt* ("Society for Space Travel") included a gifted young engineer, Wernher von Braun. He was among the many *VfR* members who were drafted to work on military rockets for Germany's Nazi Party.

Russian rocketry pioneer Konstantin Tsiolkovsky in his library. Although Tsiolkovsky went no further with his experiments than building a few wooden models, his theoretical work paved the way for the modern space age.

ROBERT GODDARD

Robert Hutchings Goddard (1882–1945) opened the way for the space age by being the first person to successfully launch a liquid-fueled rocket. A physicist with a strong interest in space travel, Goddard developed various military uses for rockets during World War I (1914–1918). In the 1920s, he became professor of physics at Clark University in Worcester, Massachusetts, where he experimented with liquid-fueled rocket engines. Goddard demonstrated the first liquid-fueled rocket in March 1926. Throughout the rest of his life, he developed steering mechanisms, on-board cameras, and guidance systems for his rockets.

Robert Goddard in his laboratory. After his 1926 launch persuaded the world to take him seriously, Goddard attracted more support and funding, enabling him to build larger, more powerful rockets that could approach the edge of space.

The Nazi rocket program continued throughout World War II (1939–1945). A team of engineers, led by Wernher von Braun, developed the world's first ballistic missile, the V2 rocket, and used it first in 1944. Even though the V2 did not help Germany win, it showed the world how far the Nazi rocket program had come. None of the other world powers had anything like it, and every country wanted it.

The last weeks before Germany's surrender saw a scramble for rocket technology between the United States and the Soviet Union (who were still allies at that time). Troops from both countries moved in to occupy Germany.

The V2 factory in Peenemünde, Germany, was closer to Soviet lines, but von Braun and his key scientists awaited capture by U.S. troops. Von Braun, the others, and some of the rockets and plans were later taken to the United States, despite the controversy over von Braun's involvement with the use of Nazi slave labor. Soviet troops, meanwhile, captured the Peenemünde factory and many staff members, eventually moving them to the Soviet Union.

The space race

The United States and the Soviet Union were both desperate for rocket technology as their uneasy wartime alliance rapidly turned into the Cold War. Both sides soon had nuclear bombs, but these terrible weapons were only a real threat if they could reach targets hundreds or even thousands of miles away. Intercontinental Ballistic Missiles (ICBMs)—more powerful versions of the V2 rocket—were the obvious solution.

Many of the scientists and engineers working on the missile programs were eager to make space

Officials of the U.S. Army Ballistic Missile Agency, pictured in 1956. Rocket scientist Hermann Oberth sits in the foreground, flanked left to right by Dr. Ernst Stublinger, Major General H. N. Toftoy, Wernher von Braun (second from right), and Dr. Eberhard Rees.

Such was the background of the space race—two hectic decades when the United States and the Soviet Union raced to prove dominance over the other in space exploration. The race began during 1955, when the U.S. announced plans to put a satellite in orbit during the International Geophysical Year, 1957–1958. The Soviet Union's announcement of plans to launch a satellite were not taken seriously.

U.S. preparations for the launch occurred in the public spotlight, which led to some poor decisions. Von Braun's team, working on missiles for the army, was sidelined. Politicians felt that a launch using an actual ICBM would send the wrong message. Instead, U.S. efforts focused on the Navy's smaller Vanguard rocket system.

While the world watched U.S. preparations with interest, it forgot about the Soviets. Soviet rocket technology was making a huge leap forward under the guidance of the brilliant engineer Sergei Korolev. He developed the R-7, with a cluster of booster rockets around its base—a huge rocket for the time.

On October 4, 1957, with no publicity, Korolev's team successfully launched *Sputnik* into orbit. The 185-pound (84-kilogram)

travel a reality, and people on both sides managed to convince their military superiors that space launches would be a valuable propaganda "weapon" in the Cold War. Although missile tests were controversial, the public in both countries was fascinated by space. In addition to its scientific value, therefore, a successful space-rocket launch would demonstrate the mastery of a powerful technology without giving up any military secrets.

SERGEI KOROLEV

Russian rocket engineer Sergei Pavlovich Korolev (1907–1966) was chief designer on the Soviet Union's rocket program through most of the era of the space race. He had been interested in rockets since childhood, but was imprisoned during the 1930s, a victim of the general paranoia that gripped the Soviet Union under its leader, Joseph Stalin (1879–1953). During World War II, Korolev worked in a scientific labor camp. Shortly afterward, he was released from prison and put in charge of the Soviet space effort. He designed the first Soviet ICBM, the R-7, the

THE ELECTROMAGNETIC SPECTRUM

Light that we see is only a small part of the electromagnetic (EM) spectrum—the mostly invisible radiation, or energy, given off by stars. Electromagnetic radiation takes the form of different wavelengths of energy as it travels across the universe. All wavelengths of the EM spectrum move at the same speed: the speed of light—186,000 miles (300,000 kilometers) per second.

The visible part of the EM spectrum, in the middle, ranges from red light with longer wavelengths, to violet light with shorter wavelengths. Beyond the visible violet light, the wavelengths become increasingly short, high-energy wavelengths that give off dangerous, ionizing, or "hot," radiation such as ultraviolet rays, X-rays, and gamma rays. Likewise, the wavelengths beyond red light become increasingly long, with lower energy levels, such as infrared (heat) waves, microwaves, radar waves, and radio waves.

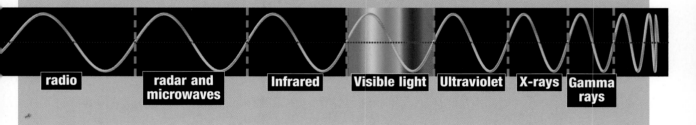

radio | radar and microwaves | Infrared | Visible light | Ultraviolet | X-rays | Gamma rays

satellite was little more than a steel ball containing a radio transmitter, but it was a propaganda triumph. As television and radio stations around the world transmitted its beeping signal, listeners were reminded that the Soviets had their own artificial "moon" in orbit. The event caused an atmosphere of near-hysteria in "free" countries. Determined to

catch up, the U.S. invited the world's press to the launch of its first satellite on December 6, 1957. The day ended in disaster. The Vanguard rocket rose just a few feet off the launchpad before the rocket fell back and exploded in a spectacular fireball.

While the media joked about the "Flopnik," the U.S. scurried to make up for lost time. Von

Sputnik satellites, and the Vostok and Voskhod spacecraft. He died during a routine operation. His last design, modified as the Soyuz capsule (intended to take cosmonauts to the Moon), is still in use today as the Soyuz workhorses of the Russian space program.

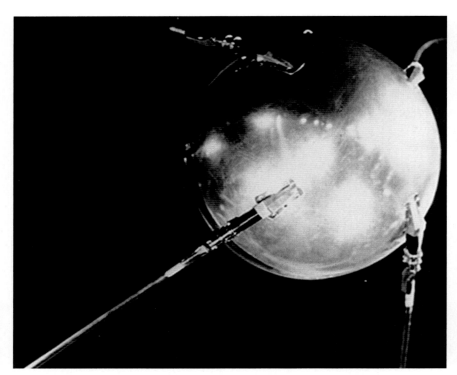

The launch of *Sputnik* in October 1957 sent the Western world into a panic: If the Soviet Union could launch a radio transmitter into space, how soon before they developed space-based weapons and spy satellites?

In 1958, the National Aeronautics and Space Administration (NASA) was created to oversee all U.S. nonmilitary spaceflights. One of their early tasks was to select America's first astronauts. Eventually, NASA settled on seven military pilots. Hailed as the "Mercury Seven"—Alan Shepard Jr., Virgil "Gus" Grissom, John Glenn Jr., M. Scott Carpenter, Walter "Wally" Schirra, L. Gordon Cooper, and Donald "Deke" Slayton—they quickly became national heroes before they ever flew in space.

The Soviet program, meanwhile, continued in secrecy. Korolev also recruited his "cosmonauts" from military pilots, but the first man in space, Yuri Gagarin, was selected for the *Vostok 1* mission partly because his family worked one of the "collective" farms touted by the Soviets as a model for the world. Moscow's authorities felt this would be good for propaganda.

Gagarin's *Vostok 1* blasted off from Baikonur Cosmodrome on April 12, 1961, on top of a modified R-7 rocket called the SL-3. The flight plan involved just one 108-minute orbit around Earth, but the impatient Soviet authorities announced the success of the mission before Gagarin's safe return to Earth. Gagarin nearly perished when his shielded, cone-shaped capsule failed to separate from the rest of the spacecraft during reentry. *Vostok 1* spun wildly out of control until the heat generated by the reentry process finally burned through the wires

Braun was confident that he could use a rocket based on his Redstone missile to put a satellite into orbit within three months, so his team was reassigned to the space program. On January 31, 1958, the U.S. launched *Explorer 1*. It returned the first information about the environment around Earth's atmosphere, including the discovery of the Van Allen radiation belts (named for mission scientist James Van Allen). *Explorer 1* was tiny (31 pounds/14 kg) when compared to *Sputnik*. By then, however, the Soviets had already launched *Sputnik 2*, which weighed 1,117 pounds (508 kg).

Humans in space

The next obvious challenge was to put a human in orbit, but the Soviets tested their spacecraft on dogs first. *Sputnik 2* carried the first animal, a small dog named Laika, who died after a few hours from stress and heat exhaustion. Putting humans in orbit would require a much heavier spacecraft, fitted with life-support equipment and shielding, in order to survive reentry to Earth's atmosphere.

Once deployed from its SL-3 rocket, Yuri Gagarin's *Vostok 1* spacecraft completed a single orbit of Earth before reentering the atmosphere as it flew back over the Soviet Union.

holding the two segments together. With the capsule back under control, Gagarin ejected as planned at an altitude of 26,000 feet (8,000 meters), and parachuted back to Earth, landing near his capsule in what is now southern Russia.

Once again, the U.S. had been beaten in the space race. NASA's new Atlas rocket needed to put a Gemini capsule in orbit was still not ready for launch, so it decided to launch Alan Shepard using the smaller Redstone rocket on May 5, 1961. Shepard's fifteen-minute flight did not put him into orbit around Earth, but his *Freedom 7* capsule reached a peak altitude of 115 miles (185 kilometers), so he became the first American in space. Gus Grissom made a similar flight aboard *Liberty Bell 7* in July 1961. By the end of the year, the Atlas rocket was finally ready. John Glenn Jr. became the first American to orbit Earth on February 20, 1962.

THE SPEED OF LIGHT

All electromagnetic (EM) radiation travels through the vacuum of space at exactly the same speed—186,000 miles (300,000 km) per second. Most often, we call this the speed of light. (What we call "light" is the visible portion of the radiation of different wavelengths that make up the EM spectrum.)

In his 1905 Special Theory of Relativity, Einstein's famous equation mathematically proved that nothing could travel faster than the speed of light. For this reason, we use the speed of light as a "constant"—a unit that never changes. One light-year is the distance light travels in one Earth year, which is roughly 6 trillion miles (10 trillion km). It is a convenient way of measuring the huge distances in space. In other words, a light-year measures distances, not time.

CHAPTER 2

JOURNEY TO THE MOON

The ultimate goal of the space race was declared before the U.S. had even put an astronaut in orbit. In a speech to Congress in May 1961, President John F. Kennedy presented America's long-term commitment to putting a man on the Moon before the end of the 1960s. It seemed absurdly ambitious to talk of sending people the quarter-million miles to our satellite at a time when no one had gone more than 196 miles (315 km) from Earth, but Kennedy knew what he was doing. NASA officials had advised him that a long race to the Moon would finally allow the U.S. to beat the Soviets in the space race.

Pathfinders to the Moon

The Apollo program—the name for the U.S. Moon missions—required an enormous commitment of time and money as well as the development of entirely new techniques for space travel. Four decades later, the Moon landings remain among humanity's greatest technical achievements. With no time to lose, NASA cut short its plans for the Mercury program and began developing its next space capsule—the two-man Gemini. The Gemini program allowed astronauts and engineers to practice many of the techniques necessary to get safely to the Moon and back, including longer-duration spaceflight, maneuvering and docking with other vehicles in space, and space walks.

Throughout this time, the Soviets were still making headlines and setting records. *Vostoks 3* and *4* went into space at the same time and flew in parallel orbits for part of their missions. *Vostok 6* carried the first female astronaut, Valentina Tereshkova. The Soviets also launched the first three-man spacecraft, *Voskhod 1*, in October 1964, and claimed the first space walk when Alexei Leonov stepped outside *Voskhod 2* in March of 1965. Behind the scenes, however, the Soviet space program

July 20, 1969: Buzz Aldrin descends from *Eagle* to take his first step on the Moon. Neil Armstrong, who had taken his historic first step nineteen minutes earlier, captured this image.

was in difficulty. Various prototype rockets proved troublesome during development, and the death of chief designer Korolev in 1966 put Soviet plans for a Moon mission further behind.

Before attempting a manned landing, NASA wanted to know as much as possible about the Moon. At the time, our satellite still had many mysteries. For example, the U.S. did not know what the far side of the Moon was like. The Soviets captured the first images of the far side, which permanently faces away from Earth, using its *Lunik 3* space probe in 1959. NASA's most important questions concerned the nature of the lunar surface. Where did the craters come from, and how widespread were they? Was the lunar soil, called regolith, strong enough to support the weight of a spacecraft? Were any areas flat enough for a safe landing?

In order to answer these questions, NASA launched an armada of lunar space probes. The Lunar Orbiters became satellites of the Moon, sending back detailed photographs and mapping the landscape in detail for the first time. The Ranger craft made "hard" landings—smashing into the lunar surface and sending back photographs up to the moment of impact.

Later, the Surveyor probes made soft landings, using rockets to slow their descent and testing the strength of the regolith.

The craters, it turned out, covered the entire surface of the Moon down to microscopic scale. This proved that the craters were caused by meteorite impacts, rather than volcanoes. Fortunately, the craters large enough to cause a problem for a lunar lander were also spaced widely apart and easy to avoid, particularly on the low-lying plains known as lunar "seas" or "maria" (singular "mare"). The regolith, meanwhile, although pounded into dust by eons of meteorite impacts, seemed stable enough to support the weight of a large spacecraft. The signs were all promising for a lunar landing.

The mission profile

How would astronauts reach the Moon and return safely? NASA realized that the Apollo spacecraft would require the largest and most powerful rocket ever assembled. Construction soon began on the giant Saturn V rockets (*see box, page 16*). Exactly how the mission itself would operate was still a mystery. NASA needed to figure out how to land an Apollo crew on the Moon, get back into Earth orbit, and finally return through the atmosphere to Earth.

A single spacecraft that could fulfill all these roles would have been far too heavy for even the massive Saturn V to launch. NASA soon settled on an ingenious system of three separate craft for different parts of the mission.

Stowed safely for launch at the top of the Saturn V, the three vehicles were, from bottom to top, the lunar escape module (LEM), the service module, and the command module. The command module was the capsule in which the astronauts would journey to and from lunar

Apollo 12 astronauts Pete Conrad and Alan Bean photographed *Surveyor 3* in 1969, thirty-one months after the probe's soft landing. The *Apollo 12* lunar module *Intrepid* sits in the background.

orbit. It was cone-shaped, with a thick heat shield on the underside. Since the astronauts would ride back to Earth in the command module, it had to survive the heat of reentry.

The service module carried life-support equipment, electronics, and the engines that would propel the entire Apollo spacecraft

and turn it around to face forward before the service module engines could be fired.

The trip to the Moon took several days, after which the main rocket on the auxiliary module fired to slow the spacecraft down and put it in lunar orbit. Two of the three crew members then climbed aboard the LEM. Once the LEM

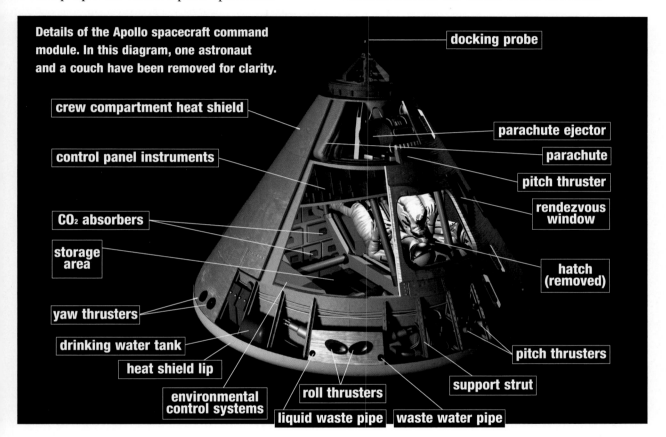

Details of the Apollo spacecraft command module. In this diagram, one astronaut and a couch have been removed for clarity.

- docking probe
- crew compartment heat shield
- control panel instruments
- parachute ejector
- parachute
- pitch thruster
- rendezvous window
- CO₂ absorbers
- storage area
- hatch (removed)
- yaw thrusters
- drinking water tank
- heat shield lip
- pitch thrusters
- support strut
- environmental control systems
- roll thrusters
- liquid waste pipe
- waste water pipe

assembly after launch. The LEM, meanwhile, was the vehicle that would actually descend to the Moon's surface. It consisted of a heavily insulated crew cabin (with a rocket on the underside to blast it back into lunar orbit for return to Earth), attached to a spidery framework of legs. The LEM had its own descent engine for braking and steering during the descent to the lunar surface.

Once the Saturn V had safely put the entire spacecraft on a course for the Moon, NASA needed to devise a way to separate the LEM from its position at the back of the spacecraft

detached from the control and service modules, retrorockets controlled its flight to the lunar surface. One astronaut remained in the command module as it orbited the Moon.

At the end of their lunar visit, the LEM astronauts fired its main engines. The blast freed the LEM's capsule from its landing gear and sent the it back into lunar orbit for a rendezvous with the command module. Once all the astronauts were safely back in the command module, the remains of the LEM were jettisoned and allowed to fall back to the Moon. As the returning spacecraft approached

Earth orbit, a final burn of the engines put it on a course for reentry. Another blast separated the command module from the service module, which burned up during reentry. Meanwhile, the command module and its astronauts plunged back into Earth's atmosphere. Parachutes slowed its descent to the surface.

The Apollo missions

On January 27, 1967, the Apollo program got off to a disastrous start. During a dress rehearsal for launch, the three crew members of *Apollo 1* were sealed inside the command module when a spark caused an electrical fire. At the time, NASA spacecraft used pure oxygen (instead of the normal mix of gases in air) inside the capsules. Flames engulfed the capsule, instantly killing the crew. NASA's engineers made a number of changes to make future flights safer. The next series of Apollo launches were unmanned tests. For eighteen months, there were no crewed Apollo flights.

NASA astronauts returned to space in October 1968, with a test flight of *Apollo 7* in Earth orbit. Later that year, a rumor spread that the Soviets planned to send a lunar mission around the Moon in early 1969. NASA moved up the *Apollo 8* launch date in order to claim this "first" during Christmastime 1968.

Apollos 9 and *10*, in early 1969, were rehearsals for a lunar landing. The *Apollo 10* lunar module descended to within 9 miles (15 km) of the lunar surface before returning to the command module and flying home.

Finally, in July 1969, everything was ready. *Apollo 11* blasted off from the Kennedy Space Center on July 16, carrying three experienced astronauts: Neil Armstrong, Edwin "Buzz" Aldrin, and Michael Collins. The flight to the Moon went perfectly, and on July 20, Armstrong and Aldrin boarded the LEM and descended to the surface, leaving Collins in lunar orbit. The only hitch in the mission came as the LEM, named *Eagle*, descended to the surface. Armstrong had difficulty finding

SATURN V

The Saturn V was the largest and most powerful rocket ever built. The Vehicle Assembly Building (VAB) at NASA's Kennedy Space Center in Florida, where these giant rockets were assembled, is still the world's largest enclosed building. The Saturn V design was patterned after the earlier Saturn I rockets originally developed by Wernher von Braun for the U.S. military.

The rocket had three separate stages. The first, 33 feet (10 m) in diameter and 138 feet (42 m) tall, had five engines that burned a mixture of liquid oxygen and kerosene. The second stage, 81 feet (24.8 m) tall, also had five engines. These burned liquid hydrogen and liquid oxygen. As each stage used up its fuel supply, it separated from the rest and fell back to Earth. The final stage was the same as the upper half of the smaller Saturn I rocket, with the Apollo spacecraft housed in a protective cone on top of it. This last stage put Apollo into a stable Earth orbit and later boosted it onto its final course for the Moon.

Detail of the Saturn V launch vehicle. Early in the Apollo program, a lower-powered version called the Saturn IB was used. The full-sized vehicle, with the giant Saturn 1C lower stage, was first used on the *Apollo 8* mission of 1968.

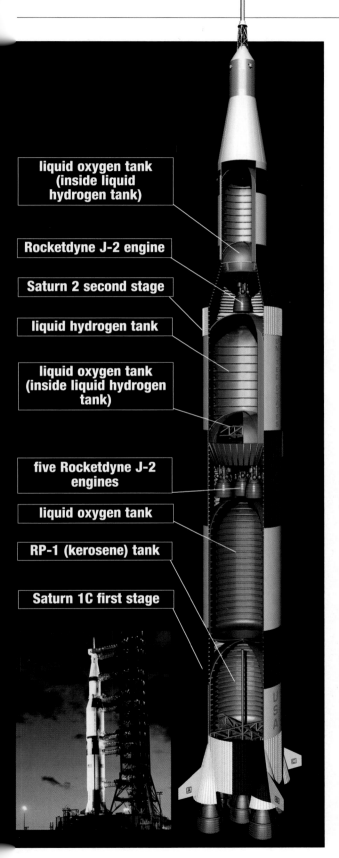

liquid oxygen tank
(inside liquid
hydrogen tank)

Rocketdyne J-2 engine

Saturn 2 second stage

liquid hydrogen tank

liquid oxygen tank
(inside liquid hydrogen
tank)

five Rocketdyne J-2
engines

liquid oxygen tank

RP-1 (kerosene) tank

Saturn 1C first stage

a smooth region for landing, and so *Eagle* touched down in the lunar Sea of Tranquillity with less than thirty seconds of fuel remaining. The world watched on live TV when, at 02:56 GMT (Greenwich Mean Time) on July 21—which in the United States, including Alaska and Hawaii, occurred on July 20 somewhere between 3:56 P.M. and 10:56 P.M. throughout the many daylight saving time zones—Neil Armstrong opened the airlock hatch, climbed down the ladder, and became the first human to stand on the surface of the Moon.

The *Apollo 11* crew did not stay long. After just twenty-one hours on the Moon, they returned to the LEM and blasted off to meet Collins in orbit and return home. Later Apollo missions grew steadily longer, with the last of the lunar astronauts spending about three days on the Moon.

Apollo 12, commanded by Pete Conrad, returned astronauts to the Moon in November 1969. This mission landed in the Ocean of Storms, close to where the unmanned probe *Surveyor 3* had landed in 1967. The astronauts located and inspected the probe to see how it had survived on the Moon.

The near-disaster on *Apollo 13* (*see page 18*) threw the Apollo program into crisis, and delayed the next launch for nearly one year. Finally, *Apollo 14*, commanded by Alan Shepard, America's first man in space, landed in February 1971 in the hilly Fra Mauro region.

The final three Apollo missions each carried a lunar roving vehicle, which was a specially built "moon buggy." It increased the area that astronauts could explore and allowed them to collect larger amounts of rock samples. The service module was also modified with new instruments to enable astronauts to study the lunar surface from orbit.

Apollo 15, commanded by David Scott, landed in July 1971 near Hadley Rille, an ancient lava channel. *Apollo 16*, commanded by John Young, arrived in April 1972 near the crater Descartes and was the only Apollo mission to investigate the heavily cratered lunar highland regions. Finally, *Apollo 17*, commanded by Eugene Cernan, landed in the Taurus-Littrow Valley. The second lunar astronaut on this mission, Harrison Schmitt, was the only trained geologist to ever walk on the Moon. On December 14, 1972, Cernan stepped back aboard the LEM for the return

Typical mission profile of an Apollo spacecraft. The complex, three-part spacecraft was the best design to reduce the amount of fuel required.

5. Upper section of LEM reunites with CSM

6. CSM jettisons LEM and flies back to Earth

7. Command module reenters atmosphere and descends by parachute.

2. Midflight docking switches arrangement of lunar module (LEM—at right) and command/service modules (CSM—at left)

4. LEM descends to Moon

3. LEM and CSM separate

1. Launch from Cape Canaveral

Jubilant technicians at mission control watch pictures of the *Apollo 13* crew's arrival on the recovery ship, USS *Iwo Jima*.

APOLLO 13

Although *Apollo 13* never made it to the Moon, it became one of the most famous Apollo missions. In April 1970, people around the world waited anxiously for news of the three-man crew after an accident during a routine test left the command module crippled and leaking oxygen into space. With no way of turning back, Jim Lovell, Fred Haise, and Jack Swigert continued into lunar orbit before swinging back and returning to Earth. In order to survive, the men climbed into the LEM (built for two) and used its limited air and power supplies for the rest of the mission. Engineers in ground control devised an emergency method for cleaning the air in the LEM. The LEM's descent engine had to put the men back on course for Earth (something it was not designed to do). The *Apollo 13* crew finally splashed down safely in the Pacific Ocean on April 17, 1970.

to Earth. He was the last man (so far) to walk on the Moon. Several countries currently have plans to return to the Moon sometime in the next two decades.

Astronaut Jim Irwin alongside the lunar roving vehicle during the *Apollo 15* mission of 1971.

OBSERVING ACROSS THE SPECTRUM

Only a small fraction of electromagnetic (EM) radiation from space reaches the surface of Earth. Although our planet's atmosphere absorbs most of the ultraviolet (UV) and some of the infrared (IR) and radio wavelengths, the visible portion of the EM spectrum makes it to the ground intact. We feel the IR radiation that penetrates the atmosphere as the Sun's heat on our bodies and other objects, while the UV rays that get through often produce skin damage, including tanning or sunburn. Still, the atmosphere also protects us from the more dangerous and damaging EM wavelengths, including X-rays and gamma rays.

We use the different wavelengths of the EM spectrum to explore space. Most ground-based telescopes scan the universe using visible light. For the clearest views, they are often located on mountaintops, where Earth's atmosphere is thinnest. On these mountain peaks, special IR telescopes also detect some of the IR radiation before the denser parts of our atmosphere block it. The best IR observing occurs from space-based telescopes, not only because of the lack of atmospheric blocking, but also because of the lack of ambient heat generated by Earth and by the IR telescope itself—which can distort images. The cold temperatures of space also require less refrigerant for cooling an orbiting IR telescope.

Earth-based radio telescopes, like the famous one in Arecibo, Puerto Rico, consist of huge metal dishes that collect long-wavelength radio waves from space. Smaller versions of radio telescopes, often built in movable groups called arrays, allow astronomers to combine many separate radio images into one larger image. Additionally, space-based radio telescopes collect and beam such data to Earth.

Space-based telescopes capable of studying the universe in different wavelengths became a reality in the decades after the launch of *Sputnik*, the world's first artificial satellite. While the famous *Hubble Space Telescope (HST)* collects images in visible light, it also carries equipment that scans the universe in IR—as does the *Spitzer Space Telescope (Spitzer)*. Space-based UV instruments include the *Hopkins Ultraviolet Telescope*, used by space shuttle astronauts, the *Cosmic Hot Interstellar Plasma Spectrometer (CHIPS)*, and the *Far Ultraviolet Spectroscopic Explorer (FUSE)* Mission. The *Wilkinson Microwave Anisotropy Probe (WMAP)* studies and maps the background microwave radiation of the universe. Space-based X-ray detectors include the *Rossi X-ray Timing Explorer* Mission, and the *XMM-Newton* and *Chandra* X-ray observatories, while the *High Energy Transient Explorer-2 (HETE-2)* Mission and *International Gamma-Ray Astrophysics Laboratory (INTEGRAL)* detect gamma-ray wavelengths. Telescopes dedicated to short-wavelength EM radiation are built to prevent these high-energy rays from simply passing right through them.

CHAPTER 3

MISSIONS AND PLANETS

Human exploration of the solar system has only gone as far as the Moon, but space probes have gone much further. The first probes to the nearby planets were another part of the space race between the United States and the Soviet Union. These missions were inexpensive compared to the lunar program and have continued for purely scientific reasons. Robotic space probes have now visited all the planets except Pluto (the *New Horizons* mission is en route) and have transformed our understanding of the solar system.

Early explorers

The Moon was an obvious target for the first space probes. As early as January 1959, the Soviet Union launched its lunar probe, *Lunik 1*. It missed its target by 3,400 miles (5,500 km), but *Lunik 2* successfully hit the Moon in September 1959. *Lunik 3* orbited the lunar far side and sent back photographs for the first time in October of that year. As explained in Chapter Two, NASA prepared for the Apollo landings with an entire fleet of lunar probes. Although the Soviet Union never put cosmonauts on the Moon, it continued sending probes there until the mid-1970s.

In the early 1960s, NASA launched its first probes, *Pioneers 5* to *9*, into interplanetary space. Escaping Earth orbit, they became independent satellites of the Sun, and sent back valuable information about conditions in space beyond Earth's immediate environment.

The next obvious targets were the nearby planets—Venus and Mars. The Soviet Union attempted to launch a Venus probe in 1961, but lost contact before the probe reached its destination. As a result, on December 14, 1962, the U.S. *Mariner 2* became the first probe to successfully reach Venus. The probe was too small to carry its own rocket engine, so it could not slow down and

An artist's impression of the *Galileo* space probe in orbit around Jupiter in the late 1990s.

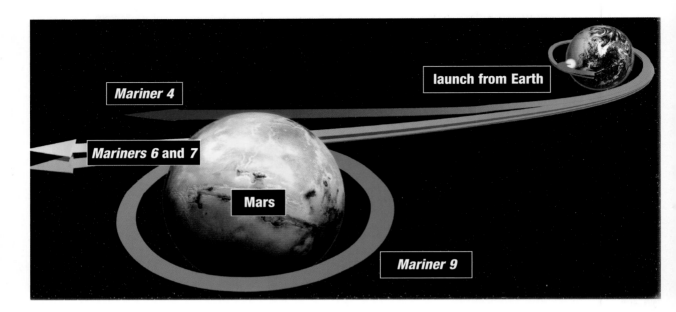

The flight paths of early Mariner missions to Mars. *Mariners 4, 6,* and *7* all flew past the planet at high speed. Only *Mariner 9* carried a braking rocket to put it into martian orbit.

enter orbit around Venus. During its brief flyby, it sent back pictures of the planet's thick yellow-white atmosphere. It also took a number of measurements of the Venusian surface temperature—which turned out to be greater than 850 °Fahrenheit (450 °Celsius).

The Soviet Union was again first to launch a probe toward Mars, but lost contact with it before it reached the target. The U.S. *Mariner 4* became the first probe to fly past Mars on July 14, 1965. In both cases, NASA benefited from its strategy of building the Mariner probes in identical pairs, so that in case of a malfunction, the mission was not totally abandoned. Two of these Mars probes, *Mariner 1* and *Mariner 3,* were lost during launch.

In the years that followed, the Soviet Union tended to concentrate on missions to Venus, while NASA focused more on Mars. In October 1967, the Soviets finally reached Venus with *Venera 4,* but an attempt to land on the surface failed because of the hostile and corrosive Venusian atmosphere. Later probes carried heavier shielding, and *Venera 8* finally returned pictures from the surface on July 22, 1967. It operated on Venus for fifty minutes before breaking down. Other probes during the 1970s and early 1980s included more landers, orbiting satellites that mapped the surface beneath the clouds using radar, and a set of atmospheric probes (part of NASA's *Pioneer Venus* mission).

NASA's *Mariners 6* and *7* flew past Mars in July and August 1969. They beamed back enhanced views of the Red Planet's surface. Because the first three Mars probes flew over Mars's cratered southern highlands, however, they missed the Red Planet's most interesting features. By 1971, when *Mariner 9* became the first probe to go into orbit around Mars and survey it thoroughly, most astronomers believed that Mars was a dead and comparatively dull world, similar to the Moon.

The pictures sent back by *Mariner 9* came as a real shock. They revealed for the first time towering volcanoes, a canyon system that dwarfs Earth's Grand Canyon, and what looked like dried-up river valleys. For the first time in years, Mars looked like a planet that could harbor simple life. The twin Viking probes soon followed *Mariner 9.* These each consisted of an orbiter that compiled a photographic atlas of the planet and a robot lander that touched down, analyzed the nearby rocks, and searched for signs of life.

An artist's impression of one of the twin Viking probes that touched down on opposite sides of Mars in July and September 1976. They returned valuable information about the martian surface and atmosphere. The results from their many experiments to find signs of microbes in the martian soil, however, remain controversial.

GETTING TO MERCURY

To date, only one space probe has sent back close-up pictures of Mercury. This tiny planet, so close to the Sun that its year lasts merely eighty-eight days, is hard to reach because of the speed with which it moves through its orbit. While Earth travels at 18 miles (30 km) per second, Mercury moves at an average of about 30 miles (50 km) per second. So, a spacecraft aiming to keep up and slip into orbit around Mercury must gain a lot of extra speed. NASA did not attempt to get *Mariner 10* into orbit around Mercury. It opted for an easier choice, putting the probe into an orbit that intersected with Mercury's orbit once every 176 days (two Mercury years). Although this allowed NASA three flyby opportunities, it also limited which areas of Mercury's surface were visible during each flyby. Detailed images exist for only 45 percent of Mercury's surface. This won't change until a probe finally manages to orbit the planet. NASA remains hopeful that the *MESSENGER (Mercury Surface Space Environment Geochemistry and Ranging Spacecraft)*, launched in 2004, and scheduled to arrive in Mercury's orbit in 2011, will finally succeed.

This photograph of Mercury is a mosaic (many images combined to make one) made from the best pictures obtained by *Mariner 10* during its three encounters with the tiny planet.

Grand tours

The first space probes to Jupiter and Saturn were *Pioneers 10* and *11*. These small spacecraft carried few scientific instruments, but they returned the first close-up pictures of Jupiter (in 1973) and Saturn (in 1979). There was a clear need for a follow-up mission, and another unique reason to launch it occurred in the mid-1970s: a rare alignment of all four outer planets. This alignment would, in theory, allow a spacecraft to fly from Jupiter to Saturn and on to Uranus and Neptune, using each planet's gravity to alter its course and pick up more speed (*see "Gravitational Slingshots" box*).

The new probes, named *Voyagers 1* and *2*, were launched in 1977. *Voyager 2* was designed as a backup to *Voyager 1*, and its main goal was to examine Jupiter, Saturn, and their moons in more detail. Although *Voyager 2*'s planned route past Saturn would take it on to Uranus and Neptune, the exploration of Saturn's giant moon, Titan, was deemed more important. If *Voyager 1* failed for some reason, *Voyager 2*'s flight path could be changed, abandoning the outer planets for a close look at Titan.

Fortunately, both spacecraft operated without a hitch. They collected a huge range of scientific data and sent back stunning images of complex weather patterns on Jupiter, the fine structure of

Neptune's moon, Triton, was a great final surprise for the Voyager missions. Neptune's varied and active moon remains a mystery, but images from *Voyager 2* hint at an icy world like that of Pluto.

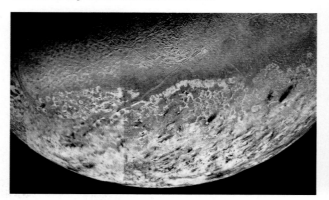

Saturn's rings, and the complex surfaces of many moons. *Voyager 1* discovered erupting volcanoes on Jupiter's moon, Io, and even a thin plane of dust around the planet—Jupiter's own faint ring.

Voyager 2 then swung around Saturn and headed out on course to rendezvous with Uranus (in 1986) and Neptune (in 1989). It provided our only close-ups of these distant blue-green worlds. Uranus proved to be a surprisingly placid world, tilted on its side (perhaps by a huge collision in its distant past). Neptune,

GRAVITATIONAL SLINGSHOTS

Gravitational slingshot or "gravity assist" is a technique used by spacecraft such as the Voyager probes to pick up speed and change direction without using fuel. The key to understanding gravity assist is to remember that all the inner planets orbit at speeds (velocities) of at least several miles (km) per second. Because planets are so large, they have enormous momentum (their mass times their velocity). One of the laws of physics states that in any encounter between two objects, the overall momentum remains the same. A slingshot maneuver allows a spacecraft to "steal" a little of the planet's momentum. The spacecraft approaches the planet from the opposite direction of the planet's orbit, gets caught up in the planet's gravity, and gains speed as it falls inward toward the planet. During this encounter with the planet, the spacecraft swings around "behind" the planet, and retreats in the same general direction as the planet's motion. From the planet's in contrast, is a remarkably stormy and active planet, with a giant moon, Triton, where geysers of slushy methane and nitrogen ice erupt at temperatures of about –390 °F (–235 °C).

Exploring the inner solar system

Except for the Voyager flybys, the 1980s were a quiet period for planetary exploration. The return of Halley's comet in 1986, however, brought together space agencies from many different countries for the first time. Halley's

comet is the only really bright and active "short-period" comet. (It is considered a short-period comet because it orbits the Sun once every seventy-six years, as opposed to other comets that have periods of tens of thousands of years.) Japan and the Soviet Union each launched two probes to study the comet's outer regions (the halo and tail), while the European Space Agency's *Giotto* mission flew within 380 miles (610 km) of the comet's solid nucleus and sent back spectacular photographs.

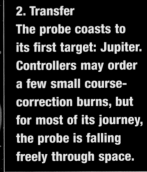

point of view, nothing has changed, but from the point of view of the entire solar system, the spacecraft gets a boost from the speed of the planet in its orbit. The planet loses a little of its own momentum as a result, and slows down very slightly.

3. First slingshot
Jupiter's gravity pulls the probe toward the planet, vastly increasing the probe's speed. The probe then swings around Jupiter and on toward its next target.

4. Second slingshot
The probe repeats its Jupiter maneuver when it reaches Saturn. Depending on the exact angle of its approach, the spacecraft can be sent inward to the Sun, outward toward Neptune, or out of the plane of the solar system altogether.

2. Transfer
The probe coasts to its first target: Jupiter. Controllers may order a few small course-correction burns, but for most of its journey, the probe is falling freely through space.

1. Launch
Usually, a space probe spends some time in Earth orbit. Controllers can check onboard systems before lining the craft up for the rocket burn that boosts it into a transfer orbit.

A panoramic color image of the martian landscape at Meridiani Planum. The Mars Exploration Rover *Opportunity* landed here on January 24, 2004. This is one of the first images beamed back to Earth from the rover shortly after it touched down.

In 1989, NASA launched *Magellan*, a Venus probe that orbited the planet between 1990 and 1994. It used an ingenious type of radar to measure the surface height, smoothness, and composition, and provided the first detailed maps of the surface of this cloudy planet.

Plans to return to Mars, however, seemed cursed. Both the United States and the Soviet Union lost probes in the 1980s and 1990s. Finally, NASA's Mars *Pathfinder* probe made a successful landing in 1997. It released a small rover vehicle, called *Sojourner*, to lumber around the surface and "sniff" the chemical composition of the rocks. In 1997, the *Mars Global Surveyor* satellite entered orbit around the Red Planet and began sending back the most detailed images yet seen. Several more probes followed, including the 2001 *Mars Odyssey* orbiter, which detected huge amounts of water ice buried just below the martian topsoil. The *Spirit* and *Opportunity* rovers that landed on opposite sides of the planet in 2004 proved that Mars once had large oceans across much of its surface. These two enormously successful rovers were still operational two years after landing.

Asteroid rendezvous

Probes were also sent to investigate some of the solar system's smaller objects. The *Galileo* Jupiter probe (*see page 28*) made the first flybys of asteroids in 1991 and 1993. The *Near-Earth Asteroid Rendezvous (NEAR),* a probe that orbited the 20-mile- (33-km-) long asteroid

RADAR

Radar allows space probes to record the features of a planetary landscape, including its changing height, roughness, and composition. The principle behind radar is simple enough. The spacecraft sends out a pulse of radio waves to a point on the ground directly beneath it, and listens for the returning echoes. Like all electromagnetic radiation, radio waves travel at the speed of light (186,000 miles/300,000 km per second), the time for the echoes to return reveals the distance to the ground. If the spacecraft's orbit is precisely known, elevation of the landscape below can be determined.

Only one factor limits the amount of detail traditional radar techniques can record: the speed at which the spacecraft itself orbits the object can produce only so many radar pulses per second, so the elevation measurements are spread out. The development of synthetic aperture radar (SAR) solved this problem. Instead of a single pulse, the spacecraft sends out a longer "chirp" of radio waves. This allows the spacecraft to detect the echoes as it travels along its orbit. A computer then processes the data to determine the elevations along a strip of the planet's surface in much greater detail.

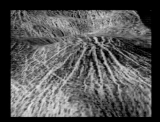

SAR images of the Venusian surface reveal details of texture, shape, and composition.

Eros for a year in 2000 to 2001, followed. *NEAR* finally touched down on the asteroid's surface in February 2001. Japan's *Hayabusa* probe scooped up material from the surface of asteroid Itokawa in 2005. Its return to Earth is planned for 2010.

A number of new missions have also been launched to comets. NASA's *Deep Impact* fired a projectile into comet Tempel 1 in 2005 and recorded the results, while *Stardust* flew behind comet Wild 2 and collected icy material from its tail, successfully returning it to Earth in early 2006. The European *Rosetta* mission will reach orbit around comet Churyumov-Gerasimenko in 2014. *Rosetta* will monitor that comet's solar approach and release a small laboratory module to analyze the comet's surface.

The *Deep Impact* projectile fired into comet Tempel 1 in 2005 produced a spectacular fountain of ice and gas from beneath the surface. Instruments on the main probe analyzed the eruption.

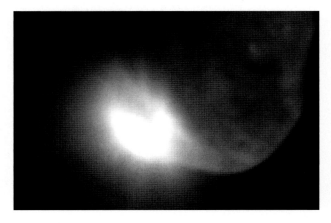

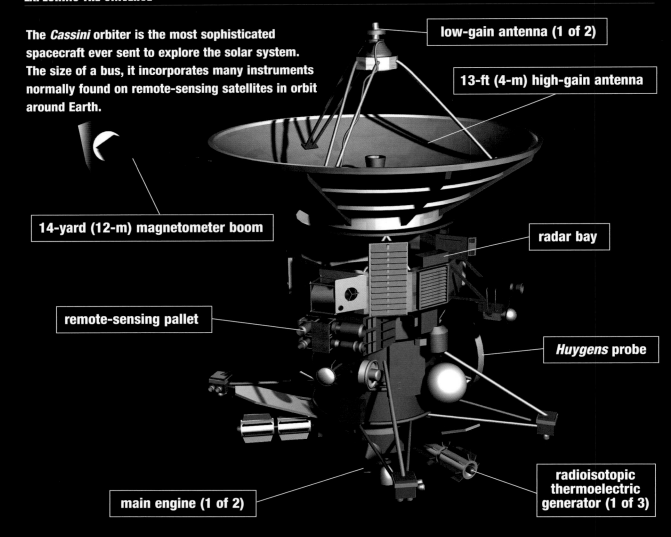

The *Cassini* orbiter is the most sophisticated spacecraft ever sent to explore the solar system. The size of a bus, it incorporates many instruments normally found on remote-sensing satellites in orbit around Earth.

low-gain antenna (1 of 2)

13-ft (4-m) high-gain antenna

14-yard (12-m) magnetometer boom

radar bay

remote-sensing pallet

Huygens probe

main engine (1 of 2)

radioisotopic thermoelectric generator (1 of 3)

There are two main reasons for this sudden interest in comets and asteroids. For one thing, scientists believe that these objects have changed little since their formation billions of years ago. They contain a record of conditions in the original "solar nebula," unaltered by the kind of chemical processes that happened on the planets. More urgently, we are now realizing the potential threat of asteroid and comet impacts on Earth. They have struck our planet in the past, causing massive devastation, and they will strike again in the future unless we learn how to divert them. A vital first step toward defending ourselves is to understand the nature of these objects and how we could best divert them from a collision course with Earth.

Intelligent explorers

The Voyager probes gave us a tantalizing glimpse of Jupiter, Saturn, and their moons, but they left astronomers wanting more. The next logical step was to send spacecraft into orbit around these two giant planets to study them up close over several years. NASA soon committed to building two new probes dedicated to fulfilling these tasks—*Galileo* and *Cassini*, respectively

Galileo, the Jupiter probe, was launched in 1989. It took six years to reach Jupiter, using a series of slingshots around Earth and Venus to put it on course. The main spacecraft had a smaller probe attached. This was a conical capsule that dropped into Jupiter's atmosphere and sent back information on the conditions there. The capsule worked well until the planet's enormous atmospheric pressure crushed it after dropping about 95 miles (150 km) below the cloud tops.

Galileo orbited Jupiter for eight years, studying the planet's atmosphere and making several close flybys of all four major moons—Io, Europa, Ganymede, and Callisto. It provided the first close-up views of Io's volcanoes, gathered evidence of an ocean of liquid water beneath Europa's icy crust, and produced puzzling evidence for something similar on both Ganymede and Callisto. Controllers used the last of *Galileo*'s fuel supplies to send it plunging into Jupiter's atmosphere. This not only provided useful scientific data, but also protected the moons from possible contamination. Europa's ocean seems the most likely place in the solar system to harbor advanced life.

Cassini was an even more ambitious probe, launched in 1997. It took seven years to reach Saturn. Like *Galileo, Cassini* carried a smaller probe, *Huygens*, with it. Built by the European Space Agency, *Huygens* was designed to investigate Saturn's giant moon, Titan. It entered Titan's hazy orange atmosphere in January 2005, deployed its parachutes, and sent back data and images as it drifted to the surface. As many scientists had predicted, Titan proved to be a world with strange similarities to Earth. While temperatures are far below freezing point on Titan, liquid methane plays the same role as water does on Earth. *Huygens* recorded methane rain in the atmosphere and sent back aerial photos of an eroded landscape, with river deltas, gentle hills, and what looks like a shoreline.

The *Huygens* probe, 9 ft (2.7 m) in diameter, attached to the underside of *Cassini* and was packed with instruments to study Titan's atmosphere and surface.

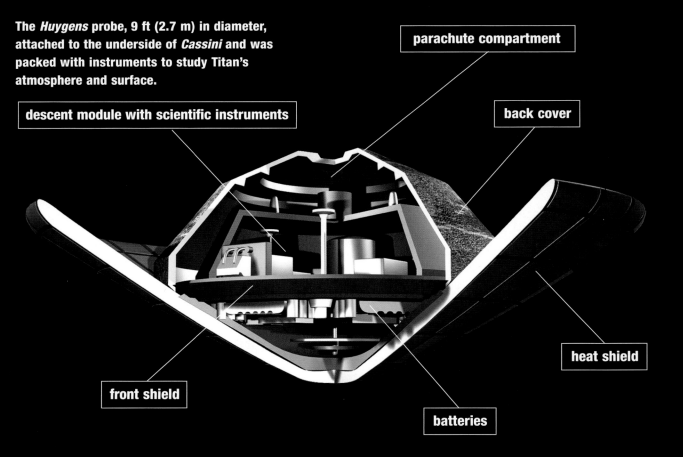

parachute compartment

descent module with scientific instruments

back cover

front shield

batteries

heat shield

STATIONS, SHUTTLES, AND SATELLITES

The Apollo Moon landings marked the end of the space race. The United States and Soviet Union decided on their next priorities and devised different plans for the future of humans in space. The Soviets concentrated on extending the stay of individual crews in orbit, building a series of space stations, while NASA focused on bringing down the costs of launch with its reusable space shuttle. At the same time, the space around Earth was becoming increasingly crowded with satellites for a variety of uses. In fact, with operational and defunct satellites, discarded rocket stages, and everything from discarded tools to flecks of paint, the hazards of space junk have increased rapidly since the 1970s.

Salyut and *Skylab*

The idea of a permanent space station in orbit around Earth had been around since at least the 1940s. Such stations have a lot of advantages. Crews can come and go in smaller vehicles and without bringing all their supplies with them. Automatic supply tugs occasionally restock the station's food, water, air, and batteries. An orbiting space station is an ideal weightless environment for carrying out experiments and provides easy access to a near-perfect vacuum. The airless conditions are great for astronomical research, and a spacecraft in orbit is a surprisingly good platform for studying Earth. (When L. Gordon Cooper, aboard his *Faith 7* Mercury spacecraft in 1963, reported seeing roads and rivers from orbit, mission control feared he was hallucinating.)

The Soviet Union launched its first space station in 1971. *Salyut 1* (the name means "salute") had a simple cylindrical design, with four segments, a docking point for a single Soyuz spacecraft, and accommodation for three cosmonauts. Only one crew member ever lived on board. The planned first crew had to abandon their mission after a docking

A space shuttle clears the launch tower during a perfect launch from launchpad complex LC-39 at Kennedy Space Center, Cape Canaveral, Florida.

problem, and the crew of *Soyuz 11* was killed when their spacecraft developed a leak as they returned home from a twenty-four-day mission.

More Salyuts soon followed. *Salyuts 2, 3,* and *5* were secret stations operated by the Soviet military. *Salyut 4* was a civilian station, and hosted two crews. One pair of cosmonauts stayed on board for sixty-three days in 1975.

At the same time, NASA briefly experimented with the idea of a space station. *Skylab* was converted from a rocket stage and was launched in 1973 using one of the giant Saturn V rockets left over from the Apollo program. Although there were some problems after launch, the first crew resolved them, and *Skylab* ended up hosting two more three-man crews, for periods of up to eighty-four days, over the next year.

In 1977, the Soviet Union launched *Salyut 6.* A leap forward in space station design, it had two docking ports. One accommodated the crew's spacecraft. Visiting spacecraft, such as the Progress supply tankers, and even temporary Star laboratory modules, used the other port. Throughout the four-year lifetime of *Salyut 6,*

cosmonaut stays got longer and the periods when the station was left empty grew shorter. The success was then repeated with *Salyut 7,* which operated from 1982 to 1986. By the time *Salyut 7* was abandoned, construction was already underway on an even bigger station: *Mir.*

The space shuttle

After the Apollo program, NASA focused on its new space shuttle. One of the major problems of space travel is the high cost of putting spacecraft and satellites into orbit. Launch vehicles that are used once and then discarded consume a large portion of the cost.

The space shuttle was designed to be (mostly) reusable. It consists of four separate sections: two booster tanks filled with solid-fuel rocket propellant; a huge external liquid fuel tank; and the shuttle orbiter itself, which is a 122-foot- (37-m-) long vehicle similar to an airplane, with three large rocket engines at the rear. During launch, these main engines draw fuel from the external tank, while the booster rockets help get the enormous vehicle moving. After about two

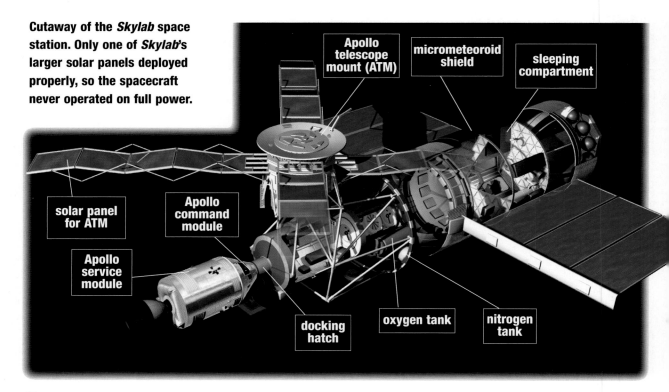

Cutaway of the *Skylab* space station. Only one of *Skylab*'s larger solar panels deployed properly, so the spacecraft never operated on full power.

Apollo telescope mount (ATM)

micrometeoroid shield

sleeping compartment

solar panel for ATM

Apollo command module

Apollo service module

docking hatch

oxygen tank

nitrogen tank

Cutaway of *Mir* as it appeared from 1996 until the end of its operating life. The ingenious modular design allowed space station construction to continue over a period of almost ten years. In this diagram, a Soyuz spacecraft is attached to the near side, and a Progress cargo ferry is attached to the far side.

MIR

The most advanced Soviet space station, *Mir* (meaning "peace"), was designed as a modular station. Once the central sections were in place, new sections, or modules (such as laboratories), could be added one at a time, gradually increasing the station's size and capabilities. The core sections were launched in February 1986, and a series of modules added over the following years. *Kvant* (1987) was an orbiting observatory for ultraviolet (UV) and X-ray astronomy. *Kvant-2* (1989) extended the astronauts' living quarters, added a shower, and carried out various experiments. *Kristall* (1990) was a laboratory for studying materials in zero gravity, while *Spektr* (1995) and *Priroda* (1996) carried telescopes and other instruments for studying Earth.

Mir remained in orbit for almost fifteen years, which was well beyond its planned life span. In that time, international politics was transformed as the Soviet Union collapsed and Russia went through an economic depression. NASA reached an agreement with the Russian Space Agency to keep the station running, and it operated with international crews until 1999. In 1995, one final module was attached to *Mir*: a docking compartment allowing visits from NASA's space shuttle.

minutes, when the boosters are exhausted, explosive bolts release them from the shuttle. Supported by parachutes for recovery and reuse, they fall back to the ocean. In another six minutes, as the liquid fuel from the main tank is starting to run out, the shuttle is almost in orbit. The main tank is released and allowed to burn up in the atmosphere, while the smaller engines of the orbital maneuvering system (OMS) push the orbiter into its final orbit.

The OMS engines, along with the reaction control system jets on the orbiter's nose section, allow the spacecraft to turn and spin in orbit. When the orbiter is ready to return to Earth, the spacecraft turns so that it is facing forward and fires the OMS engines to slow it down and drop it from orbit. From this point on, the orbiter functions as the world's heaviest glider, reentering the atmosphere at twenty-five times the speed of sound on an approach path that returns it to a landing strip in either Florida or California.

After many delays, the space shuttle *Columbia* made its first test flight in 1981. NASA initially built three more shuttles, named *Discovery*, *Challenger*, and *Atlantis*. It hoped that these spacecraft would make travel into low Earth orbit a routine, with shuttle launches roughly every two weeks. A series of problems with the insulating tiles that protected the spacecraft on reentry into the atmosphere, followed by the disastrous loss of *Challenger* and its seven astronauts in January 1986, meant the shuttle program never achieved its potential as a commercial satellite launcher.

In the wake of the *Challenger* accident, NASA built a replacement, *Endeavour*, and flights resumed in September 1988. The shuttle has, however, remained a specialist vehicle for missions that require a crew of astronauts. Shuttle crews have carried out many delicate operations in space, servicing satellites such as the *Hubble Space Telescope* (*HST*) and helping repair and build space stations. They have also carried out a wide range of experiments in the European-built *Spacelab* laboratory module (designed to fit into the shuttle's cargo hold).

The majority of satellite launches, however, are still carried out with unmanned, expendable rockets. The politicians and scientists who planned the shuttle could not have guessed at the political and economic changes that would overtake their plans as new countries entered the space industry and unmanned launches became a commercial business.

The age of satellites

People who took an interest in space exploration were predicting uses for artificial satellites long before the space age itself began. As budgets began to shrink with the end of the space race, satellites of various kinds became an increasingly important element of the space program.

A space shuttle orbiter begins its return to Earth at roughly 19,000 miles (30,000 km) per hour, rapidly losing speed as it hits Earth's upper atmosphere. The reentry process begins halfway around the world from the landing site. A series of broad "S-turns" helps the shuttle decrease its speed. During reentry, sheath of hot air around the shuttle blocks out communications for twelve minutes.

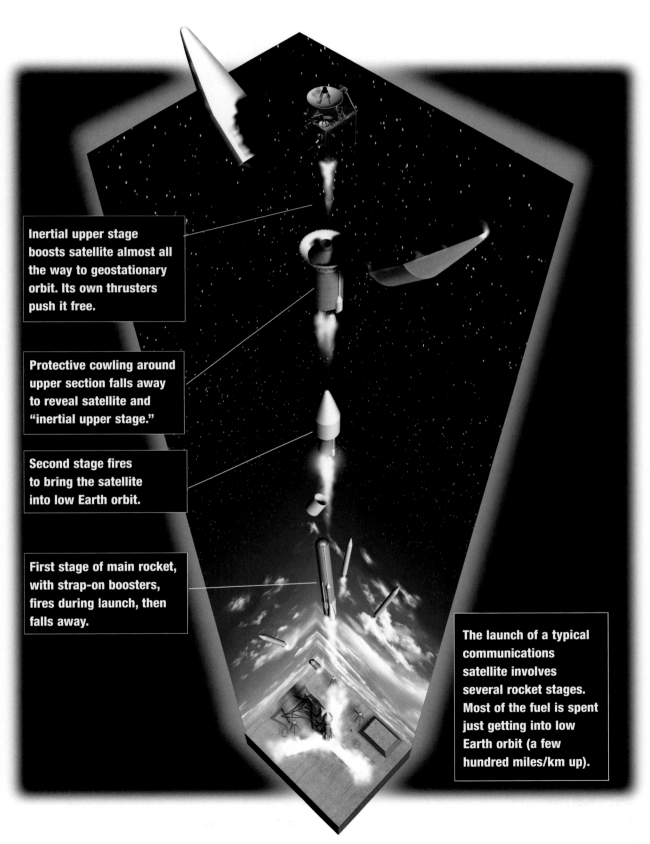

Inertial upper stage boosts satellite almost all the way to geostationary orbit. Its own thrusters push it free.

Protective cowling around upper section falls away to reveal satellite and "inertial upper stage."

Second stage fires to bring the satellite into low Earth orbit.

First stage of main rocket, with strap-on boosters, fires during launch, then falls away.

The launch of a typical communications satellite involves several rocket stages. Most of the fuel is spent just getting into low Earth orbit (a few hundred miles/km up).

Spy satellites

One of the most obvious and appealing ideas, especially in the depths of the Cold War, was the spy satellite. This was an orbiting spacecraft equipped with cameras and zoom lenses that allowed it to peer down as it flew over enemy territory, out of range of missiles or hostile aircraft. Film from the cameras could be ejected in a capsule over friendly territory, providing military intelligence. The first primitive spy satellites were the U.S. Discoverer missions, begun in the late 1950s. Although the most advanced technology is always kept out of the public eye, the equipment has come a long way since then. Pictures are now recorded in digital form and beamed back to Earth as electronic signals. Today's spy satellites can also listen in on radio communications, and can use a variety of different techniques for detecting and tracking "interesting" activity on the ground.

Earth-observing satellites

TIROS 1 (*Television and InfraRed Observation Satellite*), launched in April 1960, was the first U.S. weather satellite. Early weather satellites, like this one, had tilted orbits that only circled certain areas of Earth. Many later satellites were launched into polar orbits (*see box, page 37*), allowing them to cover much wider regions. Once rockets became powerful enough, weather satellites were also sent into geostationary orbits, giving them a permanent position over selected areas of Earth's surface. Other Earth-observing satellites use radar (*see box, page 27*), as well as a variety of other technologies, to monitor our planet, generally from low-altitude orbits.

NASA's *Earth Observing Mission 1 (EO-1)* satellite is an advanced remote-sensing satellite designed to test new technologies for monitoring Earth. Its instruments can simultaneously study Earth's landscape in various wavelengths of radiation, revealing details such as ground temperatures and vegetation cover. Some equipment can even identify diseases spreading among crops.

Communications satellites

In 1945, British science-fiction and science writer Arthur C. Clarke (b. 1917) pointed out that a satellite placed in orbit 22,300 miles (36,000 km) above the equator would circle the planet in 23 hours 56 minutes—exactly the same time its takes Earth to rotate once. The satellite would hover above one point on

ORBITING EARTH

An orbit is simply a free-fall path through space where a moving satellite or spacecraft's natural tendency to keep going in a straight line is precisely balanced by the pull of gravity toward Earth (or another massive object). Some orbits are perfect circles, but most are elliptical (stretched circles).

The most widely used orbit is low-Earth orbit—a simple circular path around Earth at an altitude of about 150 miles (240 km). This is where the space shuttle and *International Space Station* operate. Satellites launched from the shuttle are pushed up into orbits with an altitude of about 250 miles (400 km). Satellites in low orbits can fly directly above Earth's equator, but more often their orbits are inclined (tilted), so that,

as Earth rotates beneath them, they pass over different regions. Satellites are also launched into polar orbits that pass over the Arctic and Antarctic. As our planet rotates beneath them, polar satellites can scan Earth's entire surface.

Geostationary orbits (*see main text*) are used for communications and weather satellites. Because the satellite is positioned over the equator, it has a very bad view of Earth's polar regions. One way of dealing with this is to launch satellites into highly inclined elliptical orbits that pass close to Earth on one end of the orbit and farther away on the other. These satellites remain visible from one area of Earth for long periods of time. Many Russian communications satellites use elliptical orbits.

the equator and remain stationary in Earth's skies, allowing radio and microwave signals, such as telephone calls, to travel up to it and then be retransmitted to anywhere else within view of the satellite. A ring of satellites in this geostationary orbit, bouncing signals between each other as well as to and from Earth, would allow instant communications for the vast majority of the world's population.

Clarke's prediction came true. Dozens of communications satellites transmit telephone calls, television signals, and other data around the world. The only thing Clarke got wrong was the technology the satellites use. Decades before invention of the silicon chip, Clarke thought that hundreds of human operators would work routing calls through orbiting relay stations.

The first true communications satellite was *Telstar*, launched in July 1962. *Telstar* orbited far closer to Earth than a geostationary satellite, but it was the first satellite able to receive, boost, and retransmit signals. NASA finally proved that Clarke's idea worked with its series of Syncom satellites in the early 1960s. *Syncom 3*, the first satellite to reach perfect geostationary orbit, was a great success. It beamed live pictures from the 1964 Tokyo, Japan, Olympics to U.S. broadcasters. Following this success, an international organization called *INTELSAT* was set up to build, launch, and run a global network of communications satellites. Today, many communications satellites, especially for broadcasting television, are owned and operated by private companies.

Telstar 1 **was the first communications satellite. Just 170 pounds (77 kg), and only 34 inches (86 centimeters) across,** *Telstar 1* **was powered by 3,600 solar cells that provided a feeble fifteen watts of power. Nevertheless, it proved the concept and paved the way for a communications revolution.**

Navigation satellites

The principle behind navigational satellites is that the position of a satellite in the sky varies according to our location on Earth. Computerized global-positioning systems (GPS) pinpoint a position on Earth by detecting signals from a network of twenty-four satellites circling Earth. Because the signals travel at the speed of light, the time a signal takes to reach the receiver can determine the satellite's distance. A GPS receiver contains a precise computer model of the other satellite orbits. The receiver calculates its distance from three other satellites, and, because it also knows the precise location of each satellite, it determines its own position on Earth to within a few yards (meters).

Mir and *Atlantis*—working together

The late 1980s saw huge political changes around the world that had a great effect on manned space exploration. As the Soviet Union modernized and finally dissolved, the countries it left behind rapidly fell into economic crisis. Russia inherited the Soviet space program, but could not afford to operate it on the same scale as before. NASA also faced a crisis. Costs for a planned U.S. space station were spiraling, and the *Challenger* disaster cast doubt on the shuttle program. It seemed that both sides would benefit by working together instead of competing in space.

The combined global efforts resulted in the *International Space Station* (*ISS*) (*see pages 41–42*). Before construction could begin, however, astronauts and cosmonauts had to get used to working together. In a series of missions from 1995 to 1998, the shuttle *Atlantis* visited *Mir* nine times. *Mir* was fitted with a docking port adapted to allow the U.S. and Russian vessels to link. The U.S. shuttle brought equipment needed to keep the aging

space station running. Space station crews also became international, with U.S. astronauts regularly staying on *Mir* for long periods and gaining valuable experience with longer-duration spaceflight.

As the space shuttle *Atlantis* approaches the *Mir* space station, it tilts vertically before docking to the specially built docking module. In orbit together, the two spacecraft weighed 250 tons (225 tonnes)— the largest artificial structure in space until the construction of the *International Space Station.*

CHAPTER 5

INTO THE FUTURE

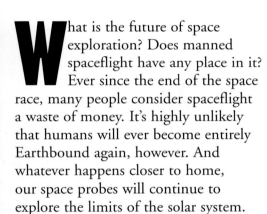

What is the future of space exploration? Does manned spaceflight have any place in it? Ever since the end of the space race, many people consider spaceflight a waste of money. It's highly unlikely that humans will ever become entirely Earthbound again, however. And whatever happens closer to home, our space probes will continue to explore the limits of the solar system.

The *International Space Station*

In 1984, President Ronald Reagan announced plans for an ambitious new American space station, to be called Freedom. His plans came at another low point in the Cold War and were linked to a space-based weapons and defense program called Star Wars. Within a few years, the reform and collapse of the Soviet Union completely reshaped global politics. Star Wars was abandoned. By the 1990s, the U.S. space station was transformed into an international project, with Europe, Russia, Canada, Japan, and Brazil contributing.

After a series of shuttle-*Mir* missions, construction of the *International Space Station* (*ISS*) finally got underway in 1998. The first phase was a shuttle mission to link the station's central hub module, called *Unity*, with the Russian-built service module *Zarya*, which provided power and life-support to the station during construction.

In November 2000, a Soyuz rocket launched the first crew to the *ISS*. Each station mission is called an expedition, and the *Expedition One* three-member crew included U.S. Commander Bill Shepherd as well as Russian cosmonauts Pilot Yuri Gidzenko and Flight Engineer Sergei Krikalev. With the crew in place, a mission by the shuttle *Endeavour* installed the first of the station's huge solar panels. When completed, the *ISS* will be the size of a soccer field, with

Artist's impression of NASA's new crewed exploration vehicle (CEV). Similarities between this spacecraft and the Apollo craft used for the Moon landings are obvious, but the new CEV will be considerably larger.

70,000 square feet (6,500 square m) of solar arrays. The U.S. *Destiny* laboratory was attached to the *ISS* in early 2002, allowing scientific work to begin.

Work on the *ISS* will include experiments in materials science that should benefit the chemical, pharmaceutical, and manufacturing industries. Crew members will test medicines that may help counteract some of the health effects of life in orbit and keep the crew in better condition for their return to Earth. The *ISS* will also serve as a platform for studying Earth in greater detail than ever before. Once finished, the *ISS* will carry a wide variety of remote-sensing instruments to monitor all aspects of our planet's environment from orbit.

Although the *ISS* has been continuously occupied since *Expedition One*, the schedule

for its completion has constantly changed—most seriously after the 2003 loss of *Columbia*, which led to the suspension of all shuttle flights. Construction should resume again in 2006, but many launches are needed to complete assembly. The *ISS* will probably not be completed until the early 2010s, and the European and Japanese experimental modules could join later still. Once the *ISS* is complete, the current plan is to retire the shuttle and rely on Soyuz capsules and new U.S. spacecraft for travel to and from the station.

The *International Space Station* in orbit above the Earth, photographed from the space shuttle *Discovery* on its 2005 visit. The *ISS* is still missing many key elements, including laboratory modules and three more of the enormous main solar arrays.

Back to the Moon—and Mars?

In the future, the *ISS* will act as an orbital base and a construction point for more ambitious missions. In 2004, U.S. president George W. Bush announced a new space strategy, ordering NASA to prepare for a return to the Moon in the 2010s and a mission to Mars some time after that.

These plans are still in their early stages, but NASA has already revealed some details of the spacecraft it plans to use. The crewed exploration vehicle (CEV) will be three times the size of the Apollo craft, combining the features of the Apollo command and service modules in a single, roughly conical, spacecraft. It will have solar panels that can deploy for more power

An artist's impression of the lander section of the new NASA CEV. The vehicle could carry four astronauts. Unlike with the Apollo missions, the command module would remain in autopilot while in lunar orbit so that all four astronauts could travel down to the lunar surface.

outside Earth's atmosphere, as well as an easily replaced heat shield that should allow reuse of the vehicle for up to ten times. The CEV could carry four astronauts at a time to the Moon. It could also link to a new lunar lander that will follow the same basic design as the earlier Apollo Moon landers.

The new spacecraft will be accompanied by new launch vehicles (*see box, page 45*). NASA's

An artist's impression of the *Mars Reconnaissance Orbiter* above the surface of Mars. The spacecraft, the most sophisticated yet to orbit the Red Planet, reached martian orbit in March 2006, after an eight-month journey. It sees surface objects that are ten times smaller than those photographed so far.

NEW LAUNCHERS

NASA's new launch vehicles are modified from the most reliable elements of the space shuttle system. The CEV will be launched on top of a two-stage rocket. The first stage is simply a modified solid-fuel rocket booster from the shuttle, and the second stage is a single space shuttle main engine fitted to a fuel tank. This combination will be enough to send the CEV into orbit for travel to and from the *ISS*. A new heavy-lift rocket will use a large main rocket stage powered by five shuttle engines, assisted by two "stretched" solid-fuel rocket boosters. This combination is capable of putting 280,000 pounds (127,000 kg) into orbit—about one-and-a-half times the weight of a space shuttle orbiter. A big safety advantage for both vehicles is that the crew or payload sits on top of the rocket. This means they are unlikely to be hit by debris falling from the rocket itself, and can be blasted free by an emergency rocket if something goes seriously wrong.

planned lunar missions include a heavy-lift rocket to put an unmanned lunar lander and an upper rocket stage in orbit. The crew would launch in a separate CEV and link up with the rest of their spacecraft in orbit, firing the upper stage rocket to put them on course for the Moon. Once in lunar orbit, they would abandon the upper stage, and all four crew members would climb into the lander for the lunar mission, leaving the CEV in orbit on autopilot. After up to seven days on the lunar surface, the crew would use the upper half of the lander (similar to the Apollo LEMs) to return to the CEV, and then travel back to Earth. The CEV capsule will land on a continent rather than in an ocean, so it can be reused.

NASA's new launch vehicles for human exploration of the solar system. On the left is the heavy-lift vehicle, while on the right is the slender launch vehicle for putting manned spacecraft in orbit.

If all goes well, NASA plans at least two of these missions every year starting in 2018, with further unmanned launches delivering equipment to help set up a permanent lunar base. This base might be sited close to the Moon's south pole, where scientists believe they have detected hydrogen (and perhaps water ice) close to the lunar surface.

The next challenge, a manned mission to Mars, will be more ambitious. Planning is still in the early stages, but the vehicles NASA plans for its Moon missions will be equally useful for Mars. Heavy-lift rockets might be used to launch parts of a Mars ship into orbit for assembly near the *ISS*, with lunar-type landers and CEVs attached to it. NASA plans to power the CEV and lander engines with liquid methane, a fuel that future astronauts traveling to the Moon or Mars might be able to manufacture during their missions.

GLOSSARY

asteroid: a rocky body that orbits a star. Asteroids vary in size from a few yards across to hundreds of miles wide.

atmosphere: the envelope of gases surrounding a planet or other celestial body.

ballistic: the path of an airborne object; also, the missile or other object launched in a controlled path that makes an arched freefall descent according to the laws of gravity.

comet: a mass of ice, rock, or dust that travels through space. Comets that pass the Sun usually develop long "tails" of gas, made up of particles defrosted or pushed away by the solar wind.

corrosive: having the power to "eat" or wear away something or to cause it to decay.

engineer: a designer or builder of engines, or a person trained in a branch of engineering, including industrial, flight, or mechanical engineering.

flyby: the flight of a spacecraft past a celestial object, often close enough for gathering data or for using that object's gravity to "slingshot" into another orbital path.

geostationary: a circular orbit directly above Earth's equator, at an altitude of 22,300 miles (36,000 km), where the speed of the object matches Earth's rotation so that the object remains in the same place (stationary) over the same point on Earth.

Greenwich Mean Time (GMT): the time set by the zero-longitude Greenwich Meridian (in Greenwich, London). GMT is five hours ahead of Eastern Standard Time in the United States.

infrared (IV): invisible form of radiation emitted by hot or warm objects; also called heat radiation.

lunar: of or relating to the Moon.

magnetometer: an apparatus used to detect the presence of a metallic object or to measure the intensity of a magnetic field.

observatory: a building designed for viewing astronomical phenomena.

pitch: movement of a spacecraft, airplane, or shuttle in which the nose and tail move up or down relative to the center of the vehicle.

probe: a device used to gather and relay information. Robot probes are used for dangerous space missions involving long flights or extreme environments.

radiation: the usually invisible energy that is transmitted in the form of waves or particles.

ultraviolet (UV): electromagnetic radiation with wavelengths shorter than visible light but longer than X-rays.

vacuum: area completely empty of matter, even air; scientists can create a vacuum artificially by pumping all the air out of a sealed space. Space is a vacuum.

vane: a sometimes moveable structure that redirects the flow of a rocket's exhaust gases to steer it and to help maintain a steady course.

yaw: the side-to-side motion of a craft that turns its nose left or right of center.

FURTHER INFORMATION

BOOKS

Bredeson, Carmen. *Nasa Planetary Spacecraft: Galileo, Magellan, Pathfinder, and Voyager.*
    Countdown to Space (series). Enslow (2000).
Graun, Ken. *Our Earth and the Solar System.* Ken Press (2000).
Hantula, Richard. *Exploring Outer Space.* Isaac Asimov's 21st Century Library of the Universe (series).
    Gareth Stevens (2005).
Kerrod, Robin. *Space Probes.* The History of Space Exploration (series). World Almanac® Library (2005).
Ride, Sally, and O'Shaughnessy, Tam. *Exploring Our Solar System.* Crown Books (2003).
Sparrow, Giles (Ed.). *The Solar System.* Thunder Bay Press (2006).
Sparrow, Giles. *Exploring the Solar System* (series). Heinemann (2001).
Stott, Carole. *Stars and Planets.* Kingfisher Knowledge (series). Kingfisher (2005).

WEB SITES

www.nasa.gov
Visit NASA's homepage and access information about the latest missions and activities.

www.space.com
Surf a great Web site for daily space news.

http://hubblesite.org/
Tour the universe with a little help from the Hubble Space Telescope.

www.seds.org
Explores the expanding role of humans in space.

http://space.jpl.nasa.gov
Choose your view the solar system from any angle or time.

Publisher's note to educators and parents: Our editors have carefully reviewed these Web sites to ensure that they are suitable for children. Many Web sites change frequently, however, and we cannot guarantee that a site's future contents will continue to meet our high standards of quality and educational value. Be advised that children should be closely supervised whenever they access the Internet.

INDEX